MAKING SENSE OF

CLIMATE CHANGE

KNOW YOUR FACTS   UNDERSTAND THE SCIENCE   WHAT CAN WE DO?

by Dr. Alex Standish

Published in 2021 by Ruby Tuesday Books Ltd.

Editors: Ruth Owen and Mark J. Sachner
Designer: Emma Randall
Production: John Lingham

Photo credits:
Alamy: Cover (top center), 21 (top left), 22 (center), 23 (bottom), 24, 25 (bottom), 27 (bottom), 29 (top); Colorado Plateau Geosystems Inc: 15 (center); Cosmographics: 5 (top), 18 (top); Creative Commons: 15 (top), 22 (bottom); NASA: 4 (top), 8 (top), 14 (right); National Science Foundation: 18 (bottom/David Noone), 19 (top/Heidi Roop), 19 (bottom/Peter Rejcek); Nature Picture Library: 13 (bottom right), 21 (center right); Ruby Tuesday Books: 6—7, 13 (top), 13 (bottom left), 14 (left), 20 (right); Science Photo Library: 17 (top), 28 (top); Shutterstock: Cover, 1, 2—3, 4 (bottom), 5 (top), 5 (bottom), 9, 10 (top), 11, 12, 15 (bottom), 16, 17 (bottom), 20 (left), 21 (bottom), 22 (top), 23 (top), 25 (top), 26, 27 (top), 28, 29 (bottom), 30—31; Superstock: 10 (bottom).

Library of Congress Control Number: 2020946939
Print (hardback) ISBN 978-1-78856-198-3
Print (paperback) ISBN 978-1-78856-199-0
eBook ISBN 978-1-78856-200-3

Printed and published in the United States of America

For further information including rights and permissions requests, please contact: shan@rubytuesdaybooks.com

www.rubytuesdaybooks.com

Contents

Earth's Changing Climate:
What's Going On?

For many years, people have been noticing gradual, but important, changes on Earth. These changes are happening because of climate change.

Shrinking Arctic Ice

The polar, or Arctic, ice cap is a vast floating island of frozen seawater in the Arctic Ocean. Each autumn and winter, it expands and grows larger. In spring and summer, it melts and gets smaller.

The red line shows the average size of the ice in September each year from 1981 to 2010.

Arctic ice September 2018

Greenland

Alaska (U.S.)

Using satellite images, scientists have been recording changes in the size of the Arctic ice since the 1970s. These images show that the ice cap is shrinking.

Some animals are struggling to adapt to climate change and other environmental challenges. In southern areas of North America and Europe, bumblebees are dying because of higher temperatures (see page 21).

A bumblebee pollinating a tomato plant

Hotter Summers & Milder Winters

In Europe there have been more frequent heat waves, such as those in the summers of 2015, 2018, and 2019. In June 2019, France experienced its highest-ever recorded temperature of 114.6°F (45.9°C) in a southern village named Gallargues-le-Montueux.

CHINA

INDIA

Indian Ocean

Maldives

A protective sea wall surrounds Malé.

Rising Sea Levels

Some islands and coastal towns are worried about being flooded or even submerged by rising sea levels. Malé, the capital of the Maldives, is an island in the Indian Ocean. It sits just 7.9 feet (2.4 m) above sea level.

Around the world, young people are voicing their concerns about climate change.

In September 2019, **millions of students** took part in protests across **150 countries.**

This book is all about making sense of climate change:

Why is the climate getting warmer?

What are the effects of climate change?

How can we adapt to our changing climate?

Can we slow global warming?

By reading this book, you will be studying climate and its effects as a **geographer**. Geographers study where things are (location), why they are there, and how they are related to other things around them. Geographers also study how people interact with the natural environment and how they adapt to different climates and landscapes.

What Do We Mean by
The Weather?

The weather varies from day to day depending on conditions in Earth's atmosphere. The atmosphere is a layer of air between the Earth and space.

Weather in Action: Temperature

The air in the atmosphere is heated by the Sun. Some parts of the globe heat up more than others. Countries on the equator, such as Brazil and Kenya, receive lots of heat all year round. In other places, such as the United States and the UK (United Kingdom), the time of year, or season, affects the temperature.

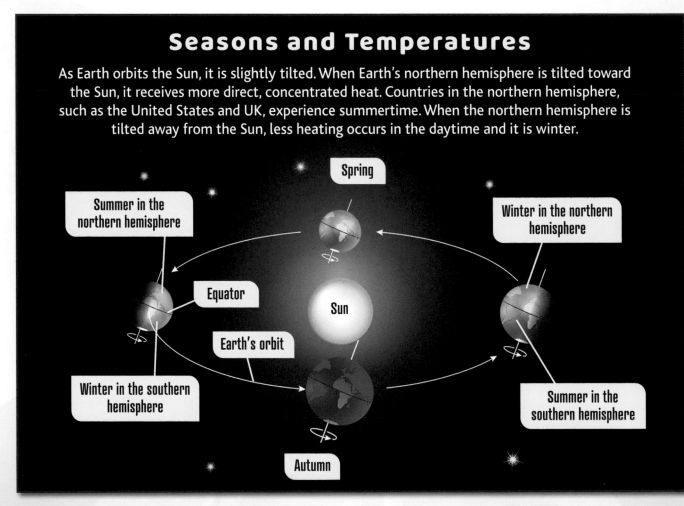

Seasons and Temperatures

As Earth orbits the Sun, it is slightly tilted. When Earth's northern hemisphere is tilted toward the Sun, it receives more direct, concentrated heat. Countries in the northern hemisphere, such as the United States and UK, experience summertime. When the northern hemisphere is tilted away from the Sun, less heating occurs in the daytime and it is winter.

Spring

Summer in the northern hemisphere

Winter in the northern hemisphere

Equator

Sun

Earth's orbit

Winter in the southern hemisphere

Summer in the southern hemisphere

Autumn

Weather in Action: Rain and Snow

Rain and snow are caused by the cycling of water between Earth's surface and the atmosphere. This is called the water cycle. Earth's water moves through the stages of the water cycle over and over again.

The **SUN** plays an important role in creating Earth's WEATHER.

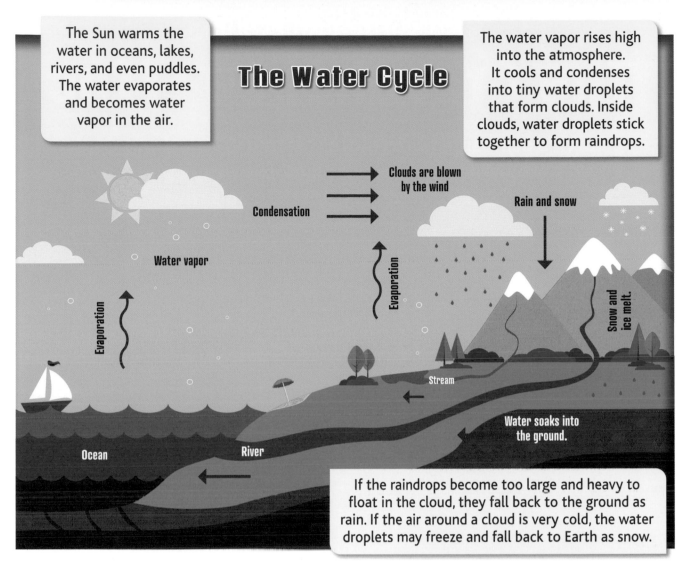

The Water Cycle

The Sun warms the water in oceans, lakes, rivers, and even puddles. The water evaporates and becomes water vapor in the air.

The water vapor rises high into the atmosphere. It cools and condenses into tiny water droplets that form clouds. Inside clouds, water droplets stick together to form raindrops.

Clouds are blown by the wind

Condensation

Water vapor

Evaporation

Evaporation

Rain and snow

Snow and ice melt.

Stream

Water soaks into the ground.

Ocean

River

If the raindrops become too large and heavy to float in the cloud, they fall back to the ground as rain. If the air around a cloud is very cold, the water droplets may freeze and fall back to Earth as snow.

Weather in Action: Wind

We call the movement of air in the atmosphere wind. Wind is produced when land or sea heats up, causing air to rise. As the warm air rises, cool air rushes into the space it has left behind, creating wind.

During a day at the beach, we often feel a breeze coming off the ocean. Why? The air above the land warms up more quickly than the air above the sea. As the warm air on land rises, cool air from the sea takes its place.

Warm Air

Cool Sea Breeze

Because nations such as Ireland and the UK are made up of islands, their weather is affected by where wind comes from.

When wind comes from the north, it is cold.

Ireland and the UK

When air comes over the Atlantic Ocean, it collects water vapor and may bring rain.

Wind coming over land (from Europe) has less water vapor and is less likely to bring rain.

When wind comes from the south, it is warmer.

7

The Greenhouse Effect

Earth's atmosphere circulates air and water that people, animals, and plants need to live. The atmosphere also helps protect us from the Sun's rays.

Atmosphere

Earth at night

What's in the Air?

Most of the air in the atmosphere is made up of the gases nitrogen and oxygen.

Nitrogen

Nitrogen is a colorless gas with no smell that is found in air, water, soil, plants, and our bodies. Plants and animals need nitrogen to help them grow.

Oxygen and Carbon Dioxide

Humans and animals need oxygen from the air to breathe. As we breathe out, we release carbon dioxide. During photosynthesis, plants absorb carbon dioxide from the air and release oxygen into the air. Carbon dioxide is also naturally released into the atmosphere when volcanoes erupt and as dead plants and animals decompose in soil.

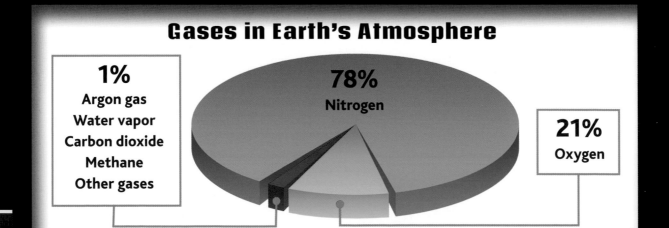

Gases in Earth's Atmosphere

1%
Argon gas
Water vapor
Carbon dioxide
Methane
Other gases

78%
Nitrogen

21%
Oxygen

The Greenhouse Gases

Other gases in the atmosphere help trap heat from the Sun and heat from inside the Earth. This heat keeps our planet warm enough to sustain life. These gases are known as greenhouse gases. They include water vapor, carbon dioxide, and methane. Without greenhouse gases, our planet would freeze!

Light from the Sun

Heat from the Earth rises up into the atmosphere.

Greenhouse gases in the atmosphere absorb some of the heat.

Some heat escapes back into space.

Heat is trapped in the atmosphere.

Without GREENHOUSE GASES our planet would FREEZE!

The Greenhouse Effect

Light energy from the Sun comes through the atmosphere and warms the surface of the Earth, producing heat energy. As the heat energy rises, some escapes into space. But some is absorbed by the greenhouses gases and stays in Earth's atmosphere, keeping the planet warm. This is called the greenhouse effect because it's a little like what happens in a greenhouse. The soil and plants are warmed by the Sun, and then the heat energy that's produced is trapped inside by the glass.

A greenhouse

Methane

Methane is a gas that is found naturally inside rocks. It's also released by animals, such as cows, when they pass wind! Methane is extracted from rock underground and is used to power boilers that heat homes and produce hot water. Some people cook with gas cookers that burn methane. This gas is also released from rotting garbage.

What Else Is in the Air?

As well as gases, there are also billions of tiny solid and liquid particles floating in the atmosphere. They include dust, pollen, smoke, volcanic ash, and salt from the sea.

What Is Climate and Climate Change?

While the weather changes from day to day, climate describes the usual weather conditions experienced at a particular place.

A Temperate Climate

In places with a temperate climate, such as the UK and other parts of Europe, winters are usually cool and rainy with occasional snow. In summer, it is usually warm and dry with occasional rain. Other climates on Earth include polar, tropical wet, and hot desert climates.

POLAR CLIMATE	TROPICAL WET CLIMATE	HOT DESERT CLIMATE

Winter in Canada

Congo rain forest, Africa

Negev Desert, Israel

A polar climate is cold and snowy with frozen ground for much of the winter. Parts of Russia and Canada have this type of climate.

A tropical wet climate is hot and humid. Rain forests grow in tropical wet climates, such as the Amazon rain forest in South America and the Congo rain forest in Africa.

This climate is hot and dry. Less than 10 in (25 cm) of rain falls each year. This type of climate is found in Israel, Mexico, and the Sahara Desert in Africa.

A frost fair on the River Thames, in London, England

Climate Change

The climate changes very slowly over decades. To see climate change in action, we need to look back over hundreds or thousands of years.

For example, in the 18th and 19th centuries, parts of Europe had much colder winters than today. It was so cold that sometimes the River Thames in London, England, would freeze over and people would organize "frost fairs" on the ice.

Global Warming

Records of air temperature show that today many places are on average 1 degree Celsius (1.8°F) warmer than they were 120 years ago. This is called global warming.

CLIMATE
is the weather in a particular place on Earth over many years.

This graph shows how Earth's temperature has risen by 1°C (1.8°F) since 1880.

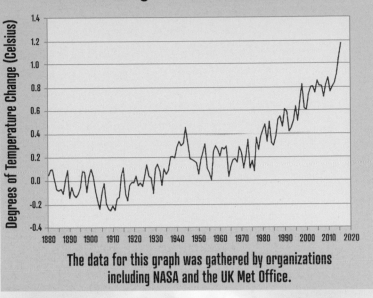

The data for this graph was gathered by organizations including NASA and the UK Met Office.

The First Thermometer

A modern thermometer

In 1714, Daniel Gabriel Fahrenheit invented the first mercury thermometer. However, thermometers were not widely used to record daily changes to the weather until the 1850s. This means that scientists only have about 150 years of recorded weather data to study.

Daniel Gabriel Fahrenheit

Daniel Fahrenheit also devised a way of measuring temperature called the Fahrenheit scale (°F). Today, most of the world uses the Celsius scale (°C).

Trees Tell a Story

Some scientists study climate by measuring the rings inside trees. Each ring shows one year of growth. In warm, longer summers, a tree grows more, so the growth rings for that period are wider. In cooler, shorter summers, there is less growth.

Warmer years

Cooler years

If a scientist counts 200 rings from the outside of a tree's trunk and sees narrow growth rings, it means the summers were cool in that area 200 years ago.

Ice Ages

If we could travel back in time thousands or millions of years, we would discover times when Earth was much colder than it is today and times when it was warmer.

What Is an Ice Age?

Ice ages happen when the Earth is much colder. Vast sheets of ice, called glaciers, spread over the land from the Arctic, Antarctica, and mountain ranges.

During an ice age, more of the planet's water is stored as ice. This causes the sea levels to drop, exposing more land. Thousands of years ago, this helped humans move from one continent to another.

The Gorner Glacier in Switzerland is more than 7.5 miles (12 km) long.

What Is a Glacier?

When snow falls in a valley between mountains, it is too cold for it to melt. As snow piles on top of more snow, it turns to ice, forming a glacier.

Ice Sheets in Europe During the Last Ice Age

Europe

The Last Ice Age

The last ice age started 1.8 million years ago and ended about 10,000 years ago. During this time there were very cold periods and milder periods when there was less ice. At its maximum, ice covered most of the UK and half of mainland Europe and North America.

The Lost Land of Doggerland

At the end of the last ice age, Britain and mainland Europe were connected by an area of land that scientists call Doggerland. It was covered with forests and swamps and was home to hunter-gatherers who migrated back and forth between Britain and Europe.

Map of Doggerland

Above sea level 10,000 years ago
Above sea level 9,000 years ago

As temperatures warmed up and the ice sheets covering the land melted, sea levels began to rise. Gradually, Doggerland became flooded and Britain and Europe became separated by sea.

Ice on Earth Today

Earth is warmer today than during the last ice age, but there are still glaciers in very high mountains, such as the Alps. The huge ice cap floats in the Arctic Ocean, and most of the continent of Antarctica is covered by an ice sheet with an average depth of 1.3 miles (2.1 km)!

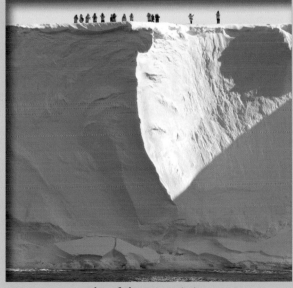

Edge of the Antarctic ice

For the last 10,000 years, we have been living in a warm period. Scientists predict that in the future there will be another ice age, but not for thousands of years.

Why Does the
Climate Change?

There are several natural processes that cause Earth's climate to warm up or cool down. These changes have been taking place since our planet formed 4.5 billion years ago, and we have no control over them.

Earth's Changing Orbit

Every 365 days, Earth makes one orbit around the Sun. But our planet's orbit doesn't always follow the same path. Scientists have discovered that over thousands of years, Earth's orbit gradually changes. It may become more (or less) oval (egg-shaped). During its history, Earth has been closer to and farther from the Sun than it is today.

Earth's orbit today

Earth

Sun

Earth

Orbit from Earth's past

With an oval orbit (such as the one shown in the diagram), the Earth spends more time each year farther from the Sun. It receives less heat and winters are longer. Scientists have linked this kind of orbit to past ice ages on Earth when temperatures were 18°F to 27°F (10°C to 15°C) cooler than today.

Solar Activity

The Sun is a giant ball of gases that produce heat and light. There are years when the Sun is more active, and times when it is less active. During more active times, the Sun sends greater amounts of energy into Earth's atmosphere, making our climate warmer. During times when it is less active, Earth receives less solar energy, so daily temperatures are likely to be slightly lower.

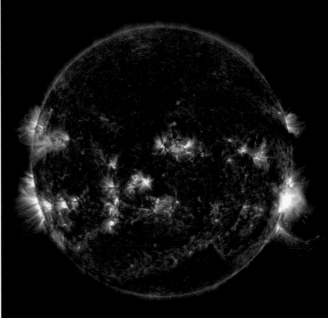

The Sun is thousands of times larger than the Earth. About 1.3 million planet Earths would fit inside our giant star.

Volcanic Eruptions

When volcanoes on Earth erupt, they push thousands of tons of gas, dust, and ash into the atmosphere. This material forms clouds that can stay in the sky for years. The clouds reflect some of the light and heat coming from the Sun back into space, slightly cooling the atmosphere.

In June 1991, Mount Pinatubo in the Philippines erupted. Scientists estimate that the clouds caused by the eruption cooled Earth's climate by about 0.9°F (0.5°C).

Mount Pinatubo's ash cloud

Continental Movements

Over millions of years, Earth's landmasses moved and changed shape, forming the continents we know today. These changes to the land and oceans affected the movement of air in the atmosphere, causing natural climate change.

Earth's Landmasses 400 Million Years Ago

Equator

The land that became the UK was here.

Rocks Tell a Story

Scientists called geologists study rocks to learn about Earth's past climate. In Scotland there is red sandstone rock that is 400 million (400,000,000) years old. The red color shows the rock contains iron oxide, which tells geologists it was formed in a hot, dry environment. When the rock formed, Scotland was nearer the equator and had a desert-like climate. Today, Scotland has a cool, wet, temperate climate.

Red sandstone cliffs in Scotland

How Have People Changed the Climate?

In the past 120 years, Earth's average temperature has increased by 1.8°F (1°C).

More Greenhouse Gases

Scientists believe that much of this global warming has been caused by people. We have added more greenhouse gases to the atmosphere, which are trapping more of the Sun's heat on Earth.

Around the world, people have been producing greenhouse gases through everyday activities that require energy.

We use ENERGY for almost EVERYTHING we do.

Fossil Fuels

Most of the energy we use is generated from coal, natural gas, and oil. Coal is a rock made out of compressed dead plants. Oil and gas formed from decaying animals and plants in prehistoric seas. Coal, natural gas, and oil are known as fossil fuels. They come from deep underground and were formed over millions of years.

Fossil fuels are powerful sources of energy. However, they are made of carbon, and when they are burned, large amounts of carbon dioxide and water vapor are released into the atmosphere.

Travel and Transportation

People like to travel! We travel daily to work and school. We travel to meet up with friends and relatives. We like to visit other countries where we can meet new people. Travel is a great way to learn about our world and different cultures.

Cars, buses, trains, planes, and boats all use energy to make them move. When they are powered by gasoline or diesel fuels (which are made from oil) this releases additional greenhouse gases into the atmosphere.

Traffic on a highway

Many homes use natural gas (methane) for heating and cooking.

A cargo ship carrying containers of goods

Generating Electricity

We use electricity to light and heat homes, schools, hospitals, and work places. We need it to print books, cook food, watch TV, power computers, and charge mobile phones. To generate electricity, some power stations burn fossil fuels, releasing greenhouse gases into the atmosphere.

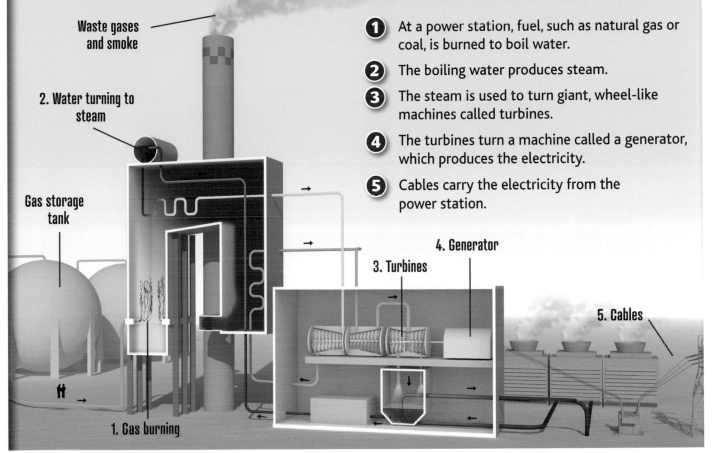

Waste gases and smoke

2. Water turning to steam

Gas storage tank

4. Generator

3. Turbines

5. Cables

1. Gas burning

1 At a power station, fuel, such as natural gas or coal, is burned to boil water.

2 The boiling water produces steam.

3 The steam is used to turn giant, wheel-like machines called turbines.

4 The turbines turn a machine called a generator, which produces the electricity.

5 Cables carry the electricity from the power station.

Industry in Our World

All the things that we use have to be made. We call the companies that manufacture these goods "industry."

The food we eat is grown on farms or produced in factories.

Growing food and making stuff produces waste. Many factories release carbon dioxide, water vapor, and other gases into the atmosphere.

Trucks, planes, and boats burn fuel as they deliver food and other goods from where they are produced to shops and our homes.

Climate Science in Action

How do we know that greenhouse gases are increasing in Earth's atmosphere?

Recording Greenhouse Gases

On the volcanic island of Mauna Loa in Hawaii, scientists have been recording levels of carbon dioxide (or CO_2) in the atmosphere since 1958.

The measurement scientists use to record the amount of CO_2 in the air is parts per million (ppm). While "percent" means out of 100, "ppm" means out of one million. Records from Mauna Loa show a rise in CO_2 from less than 320 ppm in 1960 to 414 ppm in 2020.

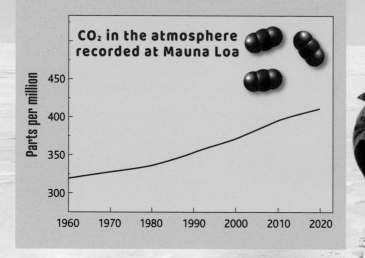

CO₂ in the atmosphere recorded at Mauna Loa

Parts per million: 300, 350, 400, 450
Years: 1960, 1970, 1980, 1990, 2000, 2010, 2020

The scientists' research shows there has been a steady rise of CO_2 in the air. They believe this increase is contributing to global warming—even though CO_2 makes up a tiny fraction of the gases in the atmosphere.

An ice core drill works in the same way as an apple corer that removes the center from a piece of fruit.

Drilling for Ice Cores

Another method scientists use to study gases in the atmosphere is drilling cores of ice from glaciers and ice sheets. The ice is made up of layers of compacted snowfall. Each year of snow leaves behind a layer of ice that contains trapped atmospheric gases from the year it was formed. The gases give scientists information about the climate that year.

Looking Back in Time

Ice core samples are drilled from the ice in sections that measure 3 feet (1 m) long. In Antarctica, scientists drill for ice cores up to 2 miles (3 km) below the surface. The layers of ice in the cores contain information about Earth's climate stretching back 800,000 years!

An ice core from Antarctica

The dark stripe is a layer of ash from a volcano that erupted 21,000 years ago.

New ice cores for storage

Metal tubes containing 3-foot- (1-m-) long ice cores

Ice core samples are stored in large freezers at laboratories.

Ice Tells a Story

The ice cores are like timelines that stretch back thousands of years. By studying ice cores, scientists can see that the amount of greenhouse gases in the atmosphere has risen in the past 100 years.

Natural or Humanmade?

Earth's climate has changed over time due to natural processes. It has also changed because people have added more greenhouse gases to the atmosphere. With both natural and humanmade processes happening at the same time, making sense of climate change is challenging.

What Changes Have We Seen as Earth Has Warmed Up?

It is difficult to predict by how much the climate will warm over the next few decades and how this will affect people's lives. However, there are some effects of global warming that people have already observed over the last 100 years.

Rising Sea Levels

Today, sea levels are rising between 0.13 and 0.14 inch (3.2–3.6 mm) per year. Since 1880, they have risen by 9 inches (23 cm). Why? As Earth's temperature warms up, ice on land in Antarctica and on mountains melts and runs into the sea. As water in Earth's seas gets warmer, it expands, causing sea levels to rise. People who live near coastlines or on flat islands are worried that their homes will eventually be flooded.

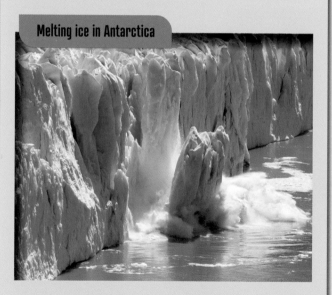

Melting ice in Antarctica

Earth's seas aren't all the same depth. So how do we know their levels are rising? A NASA satellite called Jason-3 measures sea levels from space. It does this by bouncing radio waves off the surface of a sea. Then it records how long it takes for the radio waves to return. This measurement tells scientists the distance from that particular sea's surface to the satellite. Jason-3 measures the level of every sea worldwide every 10 days, and then the data is used to track how sea levels are changing.

People on the Move?

In Bangladesh, in Asia, millions of people live on flat land near the sea. This soil is very good for farming, but as the maps show, a 3-foot (1-m) rise in sea level would mean millions of people would have to move inland. At 0.14 inch (3.6 mm) per year, it will take almost 300 years for the sea to rise 3 feet (1 m). For years, coastal areas in Bangladesh have flooded during storms. Money and expertise are needed to build better sea defenses.

Sea Level 2020 — Bangladesh

☐ Areas where millions of people live

Sea Level Rise of 3 ft (1 m) — Bangladesh

☐ Area covered by sea

More Rainfall

Some places are getting heavier than usual rainfall. Why? Scientists believe that global warming has made the water cycle stronger. Warmer temperatures cause more evaporation, which puts more water vapor into the atmosphere to fall as rain. However, the extra rain is mostly falling in places that already get plenty of rain and not in dry areas where people need it most.

Animals and Plants

As Earth's climate gradually warms, it is affecting plants and animals.

Cold water fish, such as cod and mackerel, are moving north to cooler seas as the waters where they live get warmer.

In Canada, red foxes that used to only live in the warmer south are moving north into the Arctic region. They compete for prey with the Arctic fox that has always lived in this habitat. The larger red foxes can drive the little Arctic foxes away from their hunting grounds or even kill and eat them!

This red fox has killed an Arctic fox.

Some bee species in North America and Europe have moved north to cooler areas, but bumblebees are struggling to find migration "pathways" (areas of habitat with flowering plants) to reach new habitats.

Bee habitats are destroyed by the building of roads and towns and the use of pesticides on farms that kill wild plants. Lack of habitat and food, as well as bumblebee deaths from higher temperatures, means fewer bees in fewer areas. This is a problem because bumblebees are important pollinators of plants. Thankfully, many types of bees, including honeybees, are still doing well.

Is Climate Change Causing Flooding?

After a storm, news reporters will often ask if climate change is to blame for flooding. Individual storms and flooding are caused by weather conditions at the time rather than directly because of climate change. People have also built more houses close to rivers and the coast, which means more people are exposed to flooding when it occurs. However, over the last 100 years, the average rainfall in the U.S. has increased, making flooding slightly more likely.

Damage to Crops

In the last 100 years, winter weather has become milder. Many insects that would normally die off in winter survive the cold. When spring arrives, there are more pests around ready to breed and then attack crops. In South Africa, cabbage and cauliflower crops are being eaten by swarms of moth caterpillars. In France, fruit flies have been eating olive and grape crops. There are ways farmers can manage pests. (You will learn more about this on page 23.)

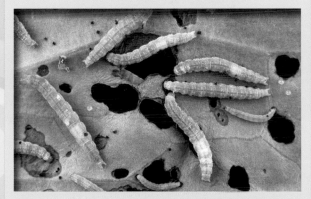

Diamondback moth caterpillars feeding on a cabbage leaf

Less Rainfall

Some dry parts of the world are receiving less rainfall than they did 50 years ago. The Sahel region in Africa is a stretch of land south of the Sahara Desert. Many of the people who live in this part of Africa farm their own land to grow food and make money. Less rainfall makes it harder for them to grow crops and raise animals.

Can We Adapt to a Warmer Climate?

Yes! In fact people around the world are doing it already.

Living Below Sea Level

The Netherlands is a country that sits on very flat land. The city of Rotterdam in the Netherlands was built on land that is 6.5 feet (2 m) below sea level. Massive sea walls and dams were built to prevent rivers and the sea from flooding the city.

The Maeslant Barrier in Rotterdam is formed from two huge floating gates. It stops water from the North Sea from flooding into the city during storms and high tides.

Defending Against Rising Seas

Low-lying countries will need to find money to build defenses to protect themselves from rising sea levels. Poorer countries may need help to fund and build the defenses they need. Experts from the Netherlands are already working in Bangladesh (see page 20) to help the country plan sea defenses that will protect people and land from flooding.

Another way to protect people and houses from the sea is to create natural places for the sea to flood into when it rises during high tides and storms. On the Scheldt River between Belgium and the Netherlands, a wetland area (marked with a red line) has been set up as an overflow area for when the river rises.

The overflow area is also a habitat for wetland animals and plants.

Managing Water Supplies

Rain doesn't always fall where we need it most. Water storage and transfer will help people adapt to a changing climate.

Solving Problems

In India, the year is divided into a rainy season (May to September) and a dry season (October to April). India is on the equator, and the temperature is warm all year round, so farmers need access to water in both seasons.

In India, people store water during the rainy season in tanks and reservoirs. A reservoir is an artificial lake made by building a dam across a valley to trap water. They also build canals to carry water from reservoirs to farms and homes where it is needed.

A canal carrying water from a reservoir in India

Sharing Solutions

In Africa, many farmers still rely on rainfall to supply their crops with water. But when the rain doesn't come, their crops may die.

To combat global warming, researchers think that governments in Africa could copy ideas from India and other countries. Money could be spent on reservoirs (which store water during rainy times) and systems to carry water to where it's needed. Then farmers would be able to grow more food and fewer people would go hungry.

Protecting Crops with Science

Warmer winters are allowing more insect pests to survive. One way to protect crops is by developing seeds that make plants less attractive to pests. Scientists do the research, and then farmers try out the new crops to see how they grow. In Malawi, in Africa, farmers have successfully grown a new variety of groundnut (peanut) that most insect pests don't like to eat.

More Adaptations for a
Warmer World

The Sahel region of Africa, which is on the edge of the Sahara Desert, is receiving less rainfall (see page 21). This is making life hard for farmers.

The Great Green Wall

A project called the Great Green Wall is aiming to stop dry areas of land from turning into desert. People in the Sahel are planting a strip of trees and crops across the entire width of Africa—that's 5,000 miles (8,000 km).

People hope this project will increase food production for people and animals. Completing the Great Green Wall will take lots of money, effort, and cooperation by people in 20 countries. The plan is to complete the wall by 2030.

Africa

People planting trees for the Great Green Wall in Sudan.

How Will Trees Help the Land?

- The trees' roots will hold onto the dry, dusty soil and stop it from blowing away.
- Leaves will fall to the ground, rot, and add nutrients to the soil, which will help crops grow.
- Rotting plant matter will make the soil better able to hold onto water when rain does fall.

Keeping Cool in Hot Weather

Towns and cities get especially hot in warm weather because the buildings, roads, and pavements absorb heat from the Sun. Trees and other plants help cool towns and cities by providing more shade and deflecting heat away from the buildings.

A New Kind of City

Masdar City in the United Arab Emirates is a new city built in the scorching hot Arabian Desert. It is an example of how people might live in a hot climate and create fewer greenhouse gases. The city is mostly powered by solar panels. Many streets are narrow and shaded for walking, and there are no cars. Underneath the city, electric pods carry people around. These pods are powered by energy that does not produce greenhouse gases.

A street in Masdar City

Green Rooftops

Some buildings have been designed to have rooftop gardens or plants growing on the outside walls. The rooftops and walls of large buildings are usually made of materials that get hot and then release heat back into the air. Plants won't do this and will help create shade on the building.

The Bosco Verticale (Vertical Forest) buildings in Milan, Italy

Designing Future Homes

There are ways to design future homes and other buildings to keep them cool if temperatures rise:

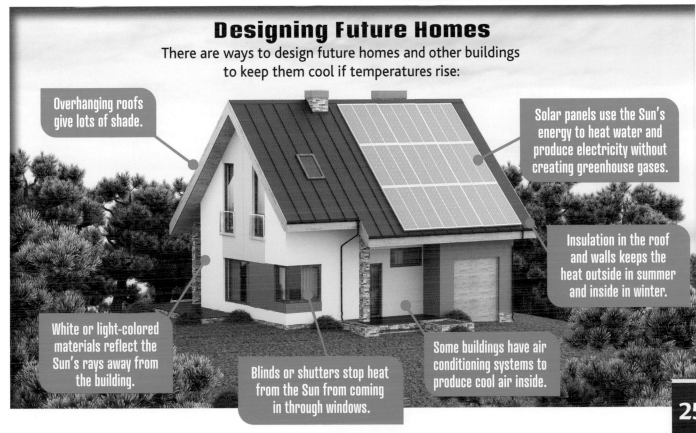

Overhanging roofs give lots of shade.

Solar panels use the Sun's energy to heat water and produce electricity without creating greenhouse gases.

Insulation in the roof and walls keeps the heat outside in summer and inside in winter.

White or light-colored materials reflect the Sun's rays away from the building.

Blinds or shutters stop heat from the Sun from coming in through windows.

Some buildings have air conditioning systems to produce cool air inside.

What Can We Do to Slow Global Warming?

Many people are concerned that the climate is warming too fast. This will cause serious challenges over the next few decades.

Big Changes

Scientists believe that we can slow global warming by reducing the amount of greenhouse gases in the atmosphere. Because the Earth and its atmosphere are so vast, small changes to how we live our lives make little difference. Slowing global warming will take change on a BIG SCALE. How do we do this?

Renewable Energy

Most of our homes, schools, hospitals, stores, and workplaces run on energy from fossil fuels that produce lots of greenhouse gases. But there are other energy sources that produce fewer greenhouse gases, including solar power, wind turbines, and hydroelectric power. They are called renewable energy sources because they are renewed by the Sun's energy.

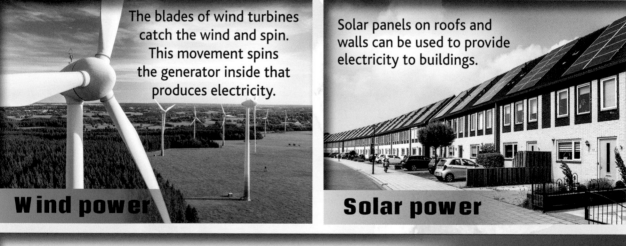

The blades of wind turbines catch the wind and spin. This movement spins the generator inside that produces electricity.

Wind power

Solar panels on roofs and walls can be used to provide electricity to buildings.

Solar power

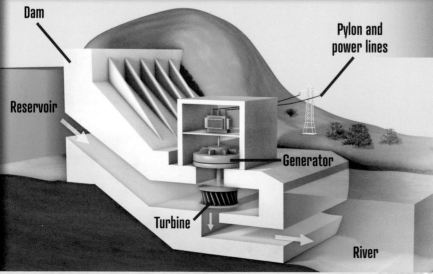

Dam

Pylon and power lines

Reservoir

Generator

Turbine

River

Hydroelectric Power

At a hydroelectric power station, water in a river builds up behind a dam and forms a reservoir. When the water is released through the dam, it rushes past the turbines, making them spin. The spinning turbines turn a generator that makes electricity.

Electric Travel

Some trains and cars are powered by electricity rather than gasoline or diesel fuel. Switching to electric vehicles is better as long as the electricity is generated without making lots of greenhouse gases. Hybrid cars use both an electric battery and a gasoline engine to travel twice the distance on one tank of gas.

An electric car recharging its battery

Better Lives, Cleaner Energy

The world's population has grown to about 7.8 billion (7,800,000,000) people. In poorer countries, people are building industry, starting businesses, and creating wealth. This means more people are buying houses, cars, computers, phones, and books. They want better food, access to clean water, education, and the chance to travel. This is good. But if the energy used to do these things is supplied by fossil fuels, it will mean more greenhouse gases and possibly more global warming. We need to find ways for people everywhere to improve their lives while using energy that produces fewer greenhouse gases.

In the future, even planes could fly using only HIGH-POWERED BATTERIES that are recharged with ELECTRICITY from RENEWABLE SOURCES.

Nuclear Power

Nuclear power is another energy source that produces fewer greenhouses gases. At a nuclear power station, a metal called uranium is split, releasing a huge amount of heat energy. The heat boils water to make steam. Then, just as in a fossil fuel power station, the steam turns the turbines that drive the electricity generators.

Inside the control room of a nuclear power station

More Ways to
Reduce Greenhouse Gases

Is it possible to remove carbon dioxide from the air? Yes!

Capturing Carbon

Oil and methane gas are mined by extracting them from tiny holes called pores in layers of rock underground. When the oil and methane are removed, the porous rock can be filled with carbon dioxide.

The carbon dioxide produced by power stations and factories can be captured before it is released through chimneys into the atmosphere. The captured gas is then transported through pipes and pumped several miles underground into rocks, where it will remain trapped. It can also be transported on boats out to sea and then pumped underground.

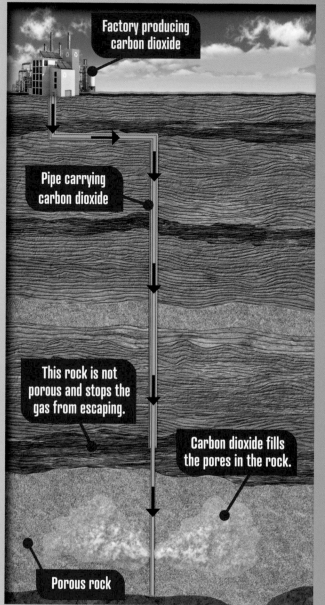

Factory producing carbon dioxide

Pipe carrying carbon dioxide

This rock is not porous and stops the gas from escaping.

Carbon dioxide fills the pores in the rock.

Porous rock

This diagram shows carbon capture in action. (The diagram is not to scale.)

Taking Care of Plants

Remember! Plants absorb carbon dioxide and release oxygen as they make their own food. Trees, bushes, food crops, grass, flowers, and even tiny cacti remove carbon dioxide from the air. This is a good reason to plant more trees, bushes, and shrubs and to protect forests, parks, fields, and gardens.

More Research and Ideas

Scientists worldwide are researching how the atmosphere and climate are changing. They study how plants, animals, and people are adapting. They also look into new ways to provide energy, such as cars fueled by hydrogen gas that produce fewer greenhouse gases.

In Switzerland, local people protect the Rhone Glacier from the Sun's heat in summer by covering it with giant insulating white blankets. The blankets reflect the Sun's light and keep heat from melting the ice.

Change Is Happening!

Remember. We need to reduce greenhouse gases in the atmosphere—but not remove them all. Since 2007, the United States has lowered its greenhouse gas emissions by 15 percent.

This is mainly because of energy production switching from coal and oil to methane gas and renewable energy sources, especially wind and solar power.

The Big Switch?

Why don't we just switch all our energy from fossil fuels to renewable sources and nuclear power?

- Renewable energy is cleaner, but it is more expensive to produce, less powerful, and less reliable than fossil fuels.

- If we make energy too expensive, more people will become poorer and struggle to buy other things they need such as food.

- If governments switch to renewable energy sources too quickly, they may not have enough money to adapt to climate change or protect their people from viruses like Covid-19.

- Wind turbines kill birds and bats.

- Nuclear power produces nuclear waste, which is very hazardous and must be safely stored for thousands of years.

When they decide which energy sources to prioritize, governments have to make decisions that balance different needs.

Join the Conversation!

What happens to Earth's climate in the future won't only depend on what humans do. It will also be affected by what happens in space as our planet orbits the Sun and our Sun has times of greater and lesser activity.

Climate Change IS Happening

Even though we don't see much change from year to year, the climate is changing—just very slowly. We do need to plan ahead to prepare for warmer seasons and changes to rainfall, and to help people and animals who will be most affected.

We Can Adapt!

Remember! People around the world already live in very different climates. They survive in the freezing Arctic. They live high up in mountains, in hot, humid rain forests, and in dry deserts. Humans are very good at adapting our lifestyles, homes, and transportation to different climate conditions. Many people cope with different weather between winter and summer. In the northern United States, you might go to school in the ice and snow of February— and just three months later make the same journey on a warm, sunny day!

°C

Learn More

Visit **www.rubytuesdaybooks.com** to find websites that will help you learn more about climate change.

Different Opinions

People have different opinions about how much of a problem global warming is causing and how best we should respond to it. You will hear some people say they don't believe it is happening. Other people will exaggerate how bad it will be.

What Do We Know for Sure?

Looking into the future, we can't be certain what is going to happen. Scientists are sure that air and sea temperatures are rising, and that these increases will have an effect on our climate. They are less certain, however, about how quickly temperatures will rise over the next decades. What happens next will also depend on what we do to slow global warming.

We Can Make a Difference

As you learn more about climate change, you will be ready to join the conversation and help others figure out how we can respond. If everybody understands the problem and helps find ways to manage it, we will be able to adapt to climate change and slow it down.

(For sources see: www.rubytuesdaybooks.com)

Share Reasons for Optimism

There are many reasons for us to be optimistic about the future.

• Across the world, fewer people are dying from all natural disasters, including those caused by weather and climate.

• An area the size of Africa (15 percent of the Earth's surface) is now protected land for wildlife.

• Today, we can produce enough food to feed everyone on the planet. Next, we need to find ways to make sure everyone has access to this food.

• Inventors have given us ways to power our buildings and vehicles that produce fewer greenhouse gases. Over time, these are becoming cheaper and more available.

• About 20 percent of the world's electric or plug-in hybrid cars are owned by drivers in the United States.

• Many countries, including the UK and United States, are reducing their greenhouse gases. Across Europe, greenhouse gas emissions are down 23 percent since 1990.

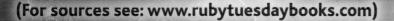

Glossary

argon
A colorless and harmless gas with no smell found in the atmosphere.

atmosphere
A layer of gases surrounding a planet, moon, or star.

carbon
A non-metal element found in all living things, but also in some rocks.

carbon dioxide
A colorless gas in the atmosphere. Its chemical symbol is CO_2, which shows it is made of one carbon atom (C) and two oxygen atoms (O_2).

equator
The imaginary line around Earth that divides Earth into the northern hemisphere and the southern hemisphere.

fossil fuels
Sources of energy (oil, natural gas, and coal) that formed from fossilized carbon sources (plants and animals) over millions of year.

glacier
A thick sheet of ice made of compacted layers of snow that moves slowly due to gravity.

global warming
The gradual increase (over many decades) of temperatures on Earth.

greenhouse effect
The trapping of some of the Sun's heat on Earth by gases in the atmosphere.

greenhouse gases
The gases (carbon dioxide, water vapor, and methane) that trap heat in the atmosphere.

habitat
The natural home or environment of a plant or animal.

hydroelectric power
Electricity generated from a turbine powered by flowing water.

ice age
A period when the Earth is much colder than it is today and ice covers some of the land.

ice core
A column of ice extracted from an ice sheet or glacier.

methane
A gas that is found naturally in rocks and from animals when they pass wind.

nitrogen
A colorless gas with no smell found in soil, plants, water, air, and our bodies.

nuclear power
Energy produced by splitting a radioactive metal called uranium.

nutrients
Substances such as nitrogen that plants, animals, and people need to grow. Plants take in nutrients from the soil with their roots.

oxygen
A colorless gas with no smell that is produced by plants. People and animals need oxygen to breathe.

renewable energy
Energy from natural sources (wind, solar, water) that are renewed by the Sun's energy and will never run out.

reservoir
An artificial lake built to store water.

turbine
A wheel-like machine that turns and generates power.

water cycle
The movement of water on Earth through its three states (solid, liquid, and gas). For example, water evaporates and floats into the sky as water vapor (gas). Then it condenses into liquid or freezes into ice (solid) and falls back to Earth as rain or snow.

water vapor
Water that has evaporated and is in the air as a gas.